Original title:
Beneath the Citrus Moon

Copyright © 2025 Creative Arts Management OÜ
All rights reserved.

Author: Riley Hawthorne
ISBN HARDBACK: 978-1-80586-463-9
ISBN PAPERBACK: 978-1-80586-935-1

Glade of Citrus Fantasies

In the orchard, fruits play hide and seek,
Lemons giggle, oranges squeak,
Limes dance wildly, up in the trees,
Making fruit smoothies with utmost ease.

Tangerine squirrels steal a slice,
Debating if it's worth the price,
They toss peels like frisbees high,
And chase each other, oh my, oh my!

Veiled Hues of Vintage Oranges

There's a rumor that oranges can sing,
When the sun sets, it's quite a fling,
With a twist and a jig, they start the show,
Vintage jokes, ripe with citrus glow.

One orange slips, it's a slippery plight,
Spinning and rolling, oh what a sight!
With laughter bursting from branches so wide,
A fruity parade, no reason to hide.

Enchanted Meridian of Tangy Glow

In the land of zest where the fruit peels roam,
A tangerine grins, making itself at home,
With a laugh it declares, "I prefer the sun!",
While grapefruits ponder what makes life fun.

Dancing with shadows in pajamas so bright,
Each citrus feels merry by the soft moonlight,
Spinning jokes like juice, they brew up delight,
In this land of citrus, everything's right.

A Citrus Night's Tapestry

Under a sky where the lemons glow,
Citrus critters put on a show,
With tiny top hats and a dash of flair,
They invite everyone to join the affair.

A lime slips, and giggles erupt,
As halved fruits form a cheerleading group,
"Three cheers for the night!" they shout in glee,
While grapefruits toss confetti for free.

Whispers of the Glistening Orchard

In the grove where lemons play,
The oranges start to sway.
Limes roll in with a cheeky grin,
Saying, "Let the juice wars begin!"

Underneath the playful stars,
Grapefruits drive their tiny cars.
Citrus charm, with a twist of fun,
Waltzing till the morning sun.

Shadows Cast by Juicy Dreams

In the shadows, fruits conspire,
Squeezing laughter like a choir.
Tangerines in a secret plot,
To wear hats, which hit the spot!

Lemons giggle, oranges sing,
Chasing squirrels, what a fling!
Under green, their jokes unfold,
A punchline wrapped in zest so bold.

The Secret Dance of Twilight Fruits

At twilight's call, the fruits unite,
Lemonade dancers twirl so light.
Kumquats bust a move so sly,
Even peaches give it a try!

In the fields, they skip and hop,
With every tumble, giggles drop.
Juggling seeds, it's quite a show,
Their humor in the breezy flow.

Luminous Nightfall Over Citrus Groves

When night falls, the zest ignites,
In a twinkling game of knights.
Lemons wear capes, oranges roar,
Squeezing juice from tales of yore!

As moonlight spills on leafy greens,
Boys and girls, in citrus dreams.
With zestful hearts, they all embrace,
A laugh-filled, fruity, merry chase.

Celestial Rinds and Dreamy Skies

In twilight's glow, a fruit parade,
Oranges dance, in twilight swayed.
A lemon juggler, quite the clown,
While grapefruits slide with comical frown.

Stars slip in the citrus cheer,
Chasing shadows, far and near.
Mandarins murmur, sweet and light,
As kumquats giggle, taking flight.

Citrus Poetry in the Night Air

The limes recite their zesty lines,
Chortling with mint, where joy aligns.
Unpeeling rhymes from orange zest,
In fruit-filled sonnets, they feel blessed.

Under the glow of playful hues,
Puns and laughs in fruity views.
A grapefruit sings a silly tune,
While lemons prank in the silver moon.

A Cascade of Citrus Fantasies

With every splash of tangy dreams,
Lemons leap and splash in streams.
A laughing lime slips on a peel,
While oranges giggle, what a reel!

Fantastical fruit, a wild delight,
Taking flight in the soft night.
Tangerines tell tales so bright,
In starlit laughter, pure delight.

The Allure of Citrus Embrace

Citrus hugs in a zesty throng,
Lemons spinning, joining the song.
Oranges whisper, "What's the joke?"
Pineapples tumble, laughter stoked.

A citrus court with jests so bold,
Fruitful tales that never get old.
As grapefruits giggle in sunny jest,
In moonlit laughter, all are blessed.

Blossoms Beneath a Mellow Glow

In a garden where limes play peek-a-boo,
The bees break dance, sipping citrus dew.
A cat in a hat, with a smile so wide,
Chases shadows, but can't catch the ride.

Lemons giggle in the gentle breeze,
As a dog tries to pick a few leaves.
A squirrel in boots, oh what a sight,
Dancing with glee in moon's soft light.

Enigma of the Sour Sunset

Oranges wear masks, like a masquerade,
Hiding their zest in a citrus charade.
A parrot quips jokes with a cheeky squawk,
While grapefruits gossip, laughing in shock.

The twilight spills juice, a tasty delight,
Puns bounce around, what a silly night!
Clouds toss confetti, bright with the fun,
As the stars join in, one by one.

Celestial Groves and Life's Zest

In a grove where fruit meets a starry dance,
Limes do the cha-cha, taking a chance.
Kiwi serenades, with a melodious croon,
While cherries tease, under the watchful moon.

Funky fruit folk gather near the brook,
With laughs that pop like a good storybook.
A pear does a split, and all cry, 'Bravo!'
While pumpkins roll by, giggling, oh no!

Golden Lanterns in an Evening Orchard

Under lanterns of gold, the fruit chit-chats,
Grapes tell tall tales of old alley cats.
A banana in glasses reads the night sky,
As a peach spins around, just gleefully shy.

Fireflies flash with a twinkle and wink,
As lemons are spotted doing the sync.
Through branches, they swing, oh what a thrill,
In a festival glow, time stands still.

The Lilt of Citrus in Starlight

In orchards bright with zesty cheer,
The lemons dance, oh what a sight!
A lizard sings, it comes so near,
While oranges twirl in pure delight.

The stars above begin to wink,
As grapefruits gossip, just for fun.
A jolly raccoon starts to drink,
Sipping punch, he thinks he's won!

The tangerines roll down the hill,
With giggles caught in the cool breeze.
A squirrel tries to steal a thrill,
But tumbles down with clumsy ease.

In this fruit grove, laughter grows,
As nectarines tease with their flair.
The moonlight bright with a glorious glow,
Makes every prank seem light as air.

Dreams of Golden Fields at Midnight

In fields where lemons softly gleam,
The critters plot in midnight's bliss.
A hedgehog wakes from sweet daydream,
While veggies cheer with a citrus kiss.

Chickens cluck in silent fit,
Stealing sips from a lemonade pool.
The fireflies dance and brightly flit,
While busy ants play hide and fool.

A pumpkin wheels with righteous glee,
While mustard plants break out in song.
The laughter spreads from tree to tree,
As nighttime antics dance along.

So join the jive and swing your hips,
In golden fields where fun ignites.
With melon shuffles and fruity flips,
The midnight joy takes flight in sights.

Under the Glimmer of Citrus Stars

Under the glow, the fruits do sway,
Dancing shadows chase the night away.
A lemon slips, a lime does roll,
In this quirky, fruity stroll.

Grapefruit giggles, loud and clear,
As tangerines all share a leer.
The oranges laugh, they start to play,
In jests of citrus, all night and day.

Soft Murmurs of Tropical Calm

Bananas whisper secrets sweet,
While coconuts plan their next retreat.
A pineapple dons a silly hat,
And swings with joy, imagine that!

Papayas chuckle, teasing fun,
As mangoes bask in the setting sun.
The playful breeze bursts through the leaves,
In laughter shared, no room for grieves.

Blood Orange Reverie

In the land where colors blend,
Blood oranges plot, and all pretend.
They tell of dreams with juicy flair,
While everything's quite unaware.

Lime spies plot a sneaky feast,
Inviting all while looking pleased.
The tartness tickles, oh what a show!
In this fruity ballet, watch them go!

Citrus Serenades at Dusk

As daylight dims, the zest takes flight,
Key limes warble into the night.
Lemons croon a soft, silly tune,
With cheers erupting from the moon.

Tangerines strut, looking so bold,
With stories of riches, not of gold.
They paint the evening with laughter and glee,
In a citrus parade, wild and free.

Whispered Secrets of Orchard Night

In the orchard, whispers play,
Fruit bats dance and kids okay.
Lemons joke with orange sprites,
As moonbeams shine on silly nights.

Crickets laugh, the breeze does tease,
While citrus dreams bring us to knees.
Fruity puns that never fade,
In this grove, the jokes are made.

The branches sway with giggles bright,
As shadows plot their funny fright.
An orange speaks, "What's the deal?"
"Why do lemons never squeal?"

So we gather, hearts out loud,
In the citrus mist, we're quite proud.
A secret world where fruit unite,
And fill the air with pure delight.

The Aroma of Twilight Citrus

Underneath the twilight sky,
Scent of zest just passing by.
Lemonade joins in the brawl,
Telling tales of summer's thrall.

Citron shimmers, sweet and bright,
Squeezed too tight, it starts a fight.
Limes poke fun, "Don't be so sour!"
While grapefruit practices its power.

A whiff of citrus fills the air,
Lemons laugh without a care.
Juicy gossip shared with zest,
In this grove, we're truly blessed.

Silly scents that swirl and rise,
Joking fruits beneath the skies.
A fragrance fresh, a fruity play,
In twilight's grip, we laugh away.

Citrus Blossoms and Starlit Journeys

Starlight sprinkles on the trees,
Fruits giggle in the breeze.
Citrus blossoms chat all night,
Tickled by the moon's soft light.

An orange twirls, a lemon sings,
While tangerines do funny things.
With every bloom, a joke takes flight,
"Let's make it a zesty night!"

Adventures called on citrus paths,
While laughing fruits share silly laughs.
A grapefruit then starts a scene,
With tales of jams and what they mean.

Beneath the stars, we spin and twine,
In this orchard, all is fine.
A journey wrapped in funny light,
Where sweetness reigns throughout the night.

A Melody of Orange and Night

In the dark, the oranges hum,
While lemons dance, they're on the run.
"Zest is best!" both fruit declare,
While grapefruits twirl without a care.

Balloons of juice float high above,
Yelling jokes, they spread the love.
Citrus melodies fill the air,
A fruity symphony to share.

The moon joins in with a cheeky grin,
As fruit folks twang their silly skin.
Laughter ripples through the vines,
With nightly tales of grand designs.

As oranges wink and lemons cheer,
We celebrate the fun right here.
A melody of taste and mirth,
In this fruit-filled, joyous earth.

Dreams Wrapped in Citrus Peel

In a land where lemons dance,
A giggling fruit takes a chance.
Oranges wear their best disguise,
While grapefruits float in silly skies.

With every squirt a chuckle plays,
They sneak and trip in fruity frays.
Tangerines roll just for fun,
What a sight when the day is done.

The limes bounce high, like rubber balls,
Chasing dreams as the laughter calls.
In this zestful, fruity spree,
Even the lime is filled with glee.

When the night brings its juicy jest,
Every citrus fruit feels blessed.
Wrapped in peels, the fun won't stop,
With every giggle, they just pop!

The Glow of Amber Night

Underneath a glowing sphere,
Limes sing songs, the night draws near.
Fruits in pajamas come alive,
In this orchard, they all thrive.

Citrus jokes fly through the air,
Bananas slip with a funny flair.
Lemon lights light up the scene,
Nighttime antics, ripe and green.

Satsumas giggle, sharing tales,
Jokes about their fruity fails.
With every laugh, a spark ignites,
Under stars, their joy ignites.

A burst of flavor, laughter spills,
As everyone gets stuck on peels.
The amber night, a canvas bright,
Painting giggles, pure delight.

The Sweetness of Twilight Juice

Twilight drips like sundrop juice,
With flavors blending, oh what use!
Lemonade rivers flow with cheer,
Full of silliness, never fear.

Grapes tell secrets, ripe and sweet,
While pulling off their clumsy feet.
Tangerines tangle in a spin,
Making chaos, shrieking, "Let's win!"

As twilight settles, fruits unite,
Creating mischief, pure delight.
Mangoes juggle, laughter streams,
In this orchard filled with dreams.

Sweetness swirls in playful ways,
As citrus smiles bright up the bays.
A punchline ripe, a scene so grand,
Fun and juice go hand in hand!

Lemon-Laced Moonlit Adventures

Under the moon, a lemon lands,
Dancing lightly, taking stands.
With zesty charm, it skips along,
Whistling out a fruity song.

Orchards echo with giggling flair,
Citrus dreams, like monkeys, dare.
Voices sweet as cozy pies,
Chase each other through the skies.

A lime rolls by, full of zest,
Tells a joke, it's simply the best.
With every chuckle, night ignites,
In the moonlight, they find their heights.

On adventures, peels are the shoes,
Grapefruit sails in his finest hues.
Together they dance, sing with glee,
Under the moon, forever free!

Gloaming Splendor Among the Trees

In twilight's dance, the squirrels prance,
Chasing shadows, they take a chance.
With acorns flying, a raucous cheer,
Who knew the woods could be so dear?

Laughter echoes from leaf to leaf,
A raccoon joins, beyond belief.
They juggle pebbles, no time to mope,
In nature's circus, there's endless hope.

Crickets play a symphony grand,
While owls hoot through the ghostly land.
A fox in a top hat, oh what a sight,
Winks at the moon, a dapper delight.

So here we gather, the merry band,
In twilight's arms, hand in hand.
With every chuckle, we boldly stride,
In gloaming splendor, we shall reside.

Cider Kisses in the Witching Hour

The clock strikes twelve, and cider flows,
With giggles mixed, as mischief grows.
Goblets raised, toasting the night,
Spooks and giggles, oh what a fright!

A pumpkin grins, with a snappy wit,
While bats above, they dare to flit.
Jugs of joy, in shadows they spill,
Sparkling laughter, such wicked thrill.

The cauldron bubbles with secrets sweet,
We dance around in whimsical beat.
With every sip, a joke we share,
Cider kisses, magic in the air.

Until the dawn, we'll play our tricks,
With every sip, a playful mix.
As morning creeps, our giggles subside,
But in the night, our joy won't hide.

Citrus Melodies in the Whispering Wind

In the orchard's glow, we hum a tune,
As lemons sway beneath the moon.
Limes laugh loud, their zest so bright,
While grapefruits join in sheer delight.

A breezy whisper through branches weave,
As playful whispers make us believe.
Mice in top hats put on a show,
In citrus realms, we steal the glow.

Orange jokes flip like circus acts,
As tangy giggles fill the tracks.
With every breeze, a prank in store,
We dance and chuckle, who could ask for more?

So gather 'round, let laughter ring,
With fruits as friends, and joy we bring.
In melodies sweet, the night conveys,
A citrus dream where mischief plays.

The Fruitful Sentinels of Nighttime

Under starlit skies, the fruits convene,
Peaches gossip, it's quite the scene.
Each berry whispers a fruity jest,
In nighttime's grip, we feel so blessed.

A melon dons a sparkling crown,
With ripe watermelon, never a frown.
The fig plays tricks, with stealthy grace,
While cherries giggle, they've won the race.

In shadowy corners, the fruits take flight,
A peach on stilts, what a funny sight!
They moonwalk softly, in playful glee,
Under the stars, so wild and free.

So join the revel, don't be afraid,
In the night's embrace, where laughter's made.
With fruitful whispers and silly schemes,
The sentinels guard our silliest dreams.

The Scent of Sun-Kissed Nights

A lemon danced with a cheeky lime,
They juggled oranges, oh so fine.
With guffaws echoed through the trees,
As starfruit giggled in the breeze.

Mango slides on a zesty floor,
Chasing zest, they all want more.
Under the glow of a playful light,
The night was ripe, a funny sight.

Tangerine tickled a grapefruit's nose,
"Knock, knock!" shouted the citrus prose.
With laughter shared in every twist,
Not one slice dared to be missed.

In this orchard of cheeky cheer,
The fruits united year by year.
A citrus choir, a silly show,
Echoing laughs as night winds blow.

Lullabies of Zesty Mornings

The sun peeked in with a citrus grin,
As sleepy fruits began to spin.
An orange yawned, a lime said, "Why?
We should wake up and reach for the sky!"

Grapes rolled over, all in a bunch,
They giggled softly over their lunch.
"We'd rise and shine, if only we could,
But oranges are sweeter in our food."

Pineapple strummed a mellow tune,
While kiwis tapped to a zesty swoon.
In every groove, a giggle laid,
A morning wake-up serenade.

As bright as peaks of zesty glee,
They pranced and danced in harmony.
With every laugh, they brought the dawn,
Spreading joy till the light was gone.

A Symphony of Citrus Spritz

The limes and lemons made a band,
A splash of zest, oh, isn't it grand?
With a citrus beat, they swayed along,
Creating melodies crisp and strong.

A pomelo solo broke through the night,
Beneath the stars, a humorous sight.
They tickled the rind, they bounced with zest,
In this spritz-symphony, life felt the best.

The grapefruit laughed with a fruity cheer,
"Let's play the tunes no one can hear!"
And the laughter rang through the tangled trees,
Fruity beats floating on the breeze.

So gather 'round, join this mad parade,
With citrus sounds that will never fade.
A juicy concert, a raucous display,
Where laughter echoes and fruits sing away.

The Dance of Clementine Spirits

The clementines twirled in their bright display,
Spinning faster, oh, what a sway!
With little giggles and joyful leaps,
They danced through gardens, in silent peeps.

A tangerine twirled with great flair,
"Can you keep up? Don't you dare scare!"
In playful jests, they all took turns,
Igniting the night with their fruity yearns.

They popped like candy, giggling loud,
Gathered together, a merry crowd.
With lemon spritz as they spun around,
In this quirky ballet, laughter found.

So raise a glass to their joyful spree,
Clementine spirits, wild and free.
In every dance, a funny delight,
Sparkling joy in the soft moonlight.

Beneath the Orange-Hued Skies

In a grove where fruit hangs low,
A squirrel wears a hat, oh no!
He's plotting schemes with peers nearby,
To snatch the snacks that humans buy.

A frog croaks jokes in lemon zest,
As bees buzz by to give their best.
The oranges roll in a silly race,
While birds above make goofy face.

Brushstrokes of Lemon Light

With a paintbrush dipped in juice so bright,
A parrot dances, quite the sight.
He splatters yellow on his toes,
While giggling at the ants in rows.

The nightingale starts a citrus song,
As limes roll by, they can't stay strong.
The moonlight turns bright fruits to stars,
While chattering critters play guitars.

Moonlit Mandarins in Flight

Tiny oranges take to air,
Chasing moonbeams without a care.
A cheeky raccoon leads the way,
"Let's fly tonight!" — he shouts with sway.

As fruits soar high, a flighty crew,
Clinging to dreams of orange stew.
They twist and twirl, in laughter soar,
Creating chaos, forevermore.

Garden of Tangy Reflections

In a garden lush with citrus cheer,
A gopher jokes, "I'll plant a pear!"
While lemons giggle in the sun,
And limes just roll, they're having fun.

A feline tries to catch a bee,
But lands in a pile of zest-filled glee.
The garden blooms with silly sights,
As fruit friends play through dreamy nights.

Citrus Echoes Against the Night

In the glow of lime and cheer,
O jester moon, lend us your ear.
We dance with fruit, so bright and round,
While giggles ripple through the ground.

The lemons laugh, the oranges sing,
Twisting tales of a citrus fling.
A grapefruit juggles, slips and falls,
Leaving us rolling by the walls.

With each bright slice, we chuckle low,
As pomelos plot a citrus show.
They reel us in with a fragrant tease,
While tangerines hang from the trees.

Under the stars, we paint the night,
With zest and joy that feels so right.
As citrus echoes fill the breeze,
Our laughter mingles with the trees.

The Lure of Sunlit Zest

In a land where zest is king,
Oranges tease and lemons swing.
Their vibrant peels distract the eye,
While we all giggle, oh my!

Citrus friends, they plot and schemed,
To make us laugh till we all dreamed.
Under sunlit skies so bold,
Silly scenes begin to unfold.

A lime does silly dances there,
While grapefruits float without a care.
Pineapples wear the finest hats,
As all the citrus chat like gats.

With every slice, we burst with glee,
Our laughter mingles with the tea.
For in this zestful, fruity space,
We find joy in every trace.

Reveries of Curdled Citrus Light

In a dream where fruits collide,
Curdled citrus takes a ride.
Lemons whirl while grapefruits yawn,
Creating chaos 'til the dawn.

Mango smiles, in pastel hues,
Claims the night, with laughs and snooze.
Fruit bats squeak, in silly flight,
Leaping high in crazy light.

Tangerines tease with every slide,
Spilling laughter, laughter wide.
Bananas flip with twists galore,
As we giggle, wanting more.

With each absurd and tangy jest,
Our fruity dreams refuse to rest.
For here in light that curls and bends,
We find sweet giggles that never end.

Tangy Whispers and Starry Dreams

With whispers of zest in the night,
Starry fruits take their flight.
Limes and lemons dance along,
While we hum a citrus song.

In the patch, a peach named Pete,
Tries to stand on wobbly feet.
Mischief twinkles in his eyes,
As laughter sprouts like bright green vines.

Grapes gossip in a fuzzy heap,
While citrus wonders make us leap.
Under the stars, their tales untold,
Leave us giggling, brave and bold.

As night drips juice and silly schemes,
We find delight in citrus dreams.
With every giggle shared in play,
We savor joy in a fruity way.

Echoes of Sunkissed Tranquility

In a garden where laughter grows,
The lemons giggle, striking a pose.
They wear their zesty hats with glee,
And dance with bees like it's a spree.

The oranges teeter, full of zest,
Claiming they're the absolute best.
With every squirt and playful splash,
The fruits conspire, oh what a clash!

A picnic spreads, a feast of shine,
Sips of juice turn dandelions divine.
As laughter spills like diverse hues,
Even the ants rush in for a snooze.

Under the glow of a chatty sun,
The fruits debate who had the most fun.
With goofy grins and silly tunes,
The garden basks in their joyous run.

When Citrus Blooms Under Starlit Skies

A tangerine winks, it knows its game,
Tomorrow's brunch will surely gain fame.
Lemons giggle, sitting so tight,
While limes play charades deep in the night.

With every whisper, a joke takes flight,
The bananas slip, oh what a sight!
Grapefruits roll, they're bold and brash,
As starry nights spread a glimmering splash.

Fruits leap and bounce in merry rounds,
Creating a circus of funny sounds.
The moon chuckles, lighting the scene,
As zest-filled antics turn nighttime serene.

Choruses of laughter fill the air,
Dancing shadows hide without a care.
An orange moon with citrus dreams,
Weaving tales sweeter than sunshine beams.

The Aroma of Nighttime Harvests

The fragrant night awakens with cheer,
As fruit revelers cozy up near.
Grapefruits gossip in secret glee,
With peels that crack like such a spree.

Mangoes flirt with the moon's bright glow,
While pears debate how to steal the show.
Every waft is a joke on the run,
As citrus cocktails mix their fun.

Harvest bees buzz, intently aware,
Of zesty jokes floating in the air.
Fruits tumble and giggle, all in a bunch,
Creating a punchline that's ripe for a crunch.

Under the laughs, the shadows play,
As citrus talks carry dreams away.
They plot the next prank, whose turn is it now?
As laughter is plotted, we take a bow.

Lemonade Skies and Midnight Whispers

A lemon sighs, 'I'm quite the catch,'
While limes join in, saying, 'Let's match!'
The skies are bleeding yellow light,
In this fruit bowl brawl, all's feeling right.

Each drop of juice, a story to swap,
As berries boast from their cozy crop.
Citrus cheers as they share their dreams,
With fizzy pops and sparkling beams.

Midnight giggles echo through the trees,
As depth of night plays with a breeze.
Jokes about seeds and tart little quirks,
The fruits surrender to playful smirks.

From lemonade skies below starry twirls,
A merry circle of fruity whirls.
With whispers of mischief in every nook,
Life is a storybook, let's share a look.

Citrus Serenade in a Silent Garden

In the garden where lemons play,
Limes joke about the end of day.
Oranges laugh with silly grins,
While grapefruits dance with tiny shins.

The moon winks at the fruit parade,
As night creatures join in the charade.
Nuts crack jokes from their tree-top stage,
While the herbs giggle, oh, what a rage!

Under twinkling stars so bright,
Forgotten berries take to flight.
With dips and twirls they pack the night,
Creating chaos, what a sight!

In this hush, a citrus affair,
With jests and quirks beyond compare.
Laughter echoes, a zestful sound,
In the garden where mirth is found.

Moonlit Secrets of the Fruitful Boughs

In the orchard where shadows loom,
Apples giggle, stirring the gloom.
Cherries whisper from their branch,
Sharing secrets, seeking the chance.

The moon hangs low, a snoopy spy,
Watching the lemons with one big eye.
With puns and tricks, they all conspire,
To ignite the night with citrus fire.

Boy, oh boy, what a fruity mess,
As tangerines don a fancy dress.
With laughter loud, they take the floor,
Dancing wildly, they crave for more.

Oh, the tales these fruits might tell,
Of silly pranks and loudfarewell.
As the moon grins from its perch up high,
The harvest jests until they sigh.

Glistening Orbs in the Night's Embrace

Citrus orbs, with shiny skins,
Rolling 'round and making spins.
They tumble down, no cares, no fuss,
While starry skies just laugh at us.

Nights filled with sweet and sour jokes,
Tangerines perform with pokes.
The nectarines throw comical fits,
While lemons crack the zaniest wits.

Every glimmer holds a fun surprise,
As limes exchange ridiculous highs.
In this chaos, friendships bloom,
Underneath that sparkly gloom.

And as the moon begins to fade,
The fruits unite in a grand parade.
With giggles bright, they bid goodbye,
As dawn approaches, painting the sky.

A Tapestry Woven with Zesty Dreams

In a world where zest is king,
Oranges plot a wild swing.
With build-up to a juicy joke,
Bananas laugh till they nearly choke.

The moon drapes colors bold and funny,
While berries dance, all warm and sunny.
With every twist, they knit a tale,
Of citrus mischief without fail.

Underneath the silent stars,
Peaches giggle, oh, how bizarre!
They turn their skins in hues so bright,
Setting the stage for the comedic night.

Each fruit glows with a playful scheme,
Woven in laughter, stitched with dream.
As morning breaks, they chuckle low,
In this tapestry of fruity show.

Glowing Lanterns in the Lemon Orchard

In the orchard where lemons glow,
Lanterns dance in a silly row.
Critters wear hats, feeling spry,
As they giggle and swoop by.

A parrot croaks a wobbly tune,
While the raccoons break out a spoon.
Sipping lemonade, what a sight,
Toasts to the moon, laughter ignites!

Frogs in bowties are having a ball,
While fireflies twinkle above them all.
With citrus jokes, the night feels bright,
In this zesty, whimsical light!

Grapefruit glares at the playful crew,
"Stop bouncing on lemons!" they laugh and boo.
With a giggle, they shimmy and sway,
In their sweet orchard ballet!

Twilight Shadows and Zesty Tales

Under twilight, shadows play,
Zesty tales have come to stay.
Lemons gossip in the breeze,
While lizards lounge beneath the trees.

A cat with a squishy lemon hat,
Tells the tale of a dancing rat.
They jive under starlit skies,
While locals laugh, not even shy!

The oranges roll, a race begins,
In orange peels, they wear their wins.
"I'm the juiciest!" they all cry,
While lemons wink with a sly reply!

At dusk, the night brings cheeky fun,
Beneath a moonlit zest, we run.
With a sip of fizz, oh what a thrill,
In the orchard, we laugh and spill!

Slices of Nightfall's Citrus Glow

The nightfall brings a citrus cheer,
With glowing slices, we all draw near.
Lemons play cards, fruity and bright,
While limes critique the amateur light.

Chickens cluck at the tales they weave,
Beneath a moon, none can believe.
"Citrus crimes!" they squawk and peep,
As a grapefruit rolls, it's time for sleep!

Bananas slip, a comedic glide,
As lemons burst from the party's side.
Jokes fly around like zippy beams,
In this fruitful land of silly dreams!

In citrus coats, we dance 'til dawn,
With laughter's echo, our fears are gone.
In this zesty realm, fun never ends,
As we share a laugh with all our friends!

Luminous Trails of Lemon Blossom

In gardens where blossoms shine at night,
Lemon trails lead us toward delight.
A bunny with glasses reads a chart,
Guiding the crew with a silly start.

Squirrels are juggling tangy spheres,
While fireflies dance, shaking off fears.
With sweet refrains, the night unfolds,
This zesty adventure never gets old!

A toad on a scooter zooms by fast,
"This is the best party!" he shouts at last.
While citrus scents fill the air so sweet,
Laughter rings out in this lively beat!

We waltz amidst the yellow blooms,
Chasing giggles through fragrant rooms.
Under glowing stars, we twist and spin,
In our lemon land, let the fun begin!

Twilight Tales of Glimmering Groves

In the grove where shadows dance,
Lemons joke, they take a chance.
Limes throw parties, quite a spree,
While grapefruits roll, so carelessly.

Citrus laughter fills the air,
Mandarins play truth or dare.
With orange hats and zestful cheer,
They giggle softly, far and near.

Night wears its brightest smile tonight,
Glow of fruits, a comical sight.
Chasing fireflies, having fun,
Joking 'bout the morning sun.

So grab a fruit, come take a seat,
Join the party, feel the beat.
In these groves, where joy imparts,
The sweetest giggles fill our hearts.

Harvest Moon and Citrusy Whispers

Under a moon that winks and glows,
Fruits wear hats with funny bows.
Tangerines tell tales of old,
About the nights that never cold.

The pumpkin giggles, soft and round,
While lemons play on merry ground.
Citrus quirks, oh what a sight,
As they dance into the night.

Limes wear sunglasses, oh so cool,
While grapefruits swim in the pool.
In this laughter-filled brigade,
Even oranges try to parade.

Join the fun, don't miss the show,
In this grove, the chuckles flow.
With every fruit, a laugh we grow,
Harvest bright beneath the glow.

When Stars Guise the Orchard's Splendor

Stars wear costumes, looking bright,
Whilst apples giggle in delight.
Peaches toss confetti high,
While cherries cheer, oh me, oh my!

Underneath the sparkling skies,
Pineapples dance, to no surprise.
Bananas slip, but do not fall,
With every slip, they have a ball.

Apricots form a funny choir,
Singing songs around the fire.
What a sight, this fruity show,
As the stars begin to glow.

With laughter loud, this night is fine,
Each fruit a star, each joke a line.
In this orchard, joy is free,
Where every bite brings glee, you see!

Whispers of Tangerine Twilight

Tangerine tales on whispering breeze,
Fruits cozied up, doing as they please.
Lemons gossip; oh, what a scene,
While joyfully rolling, friends convene.

In twilight's hue, the grapes confide,
"Did you hear? The peach has tried to hide!"
Melons laugh, they cannot keep still,
As oranges plot a fruity thrill.

Under starlight, laughter swells,
Zesty tales that everyone tells.
With zany dances, fruits unite,
Creating lore that feels just right.

So raise a toast to citrus sway,
In this twilight, let's laugh and play.
With every nibble, let joy bloom,
As we celebrate our fruity loom.

Pomegranate Lanterns and Chilling Zephyrs

In gardens where fruit clowns dance,
Pomegranates giggle, take a chance.
The zephyrs whisper silly tunes,
While squirrels wear hats made of prunes.

Trees sway like they're at a ball,
With oranges that bounce and roll.
A lemon drops its zesty grin,
And grapefruit shimmies, joining in!

Under stars that sparkle bright,
Mocking shadows leap with delight.
The moon sneezes, cheers, and then
Applauds the antics of the men.

So let us laugh with the night air,
As citrus fruits dance without a care.
Create a jamboree so loud,
That all the sleepyheads feel proud!

Silhouettes of Sweetness at Dusk

At twilight when the lemons yawn,
Grapefruit pickles play on the lawn.
Strawberries twirl in fluffy socks,
While peach pie dreams climb lemon rocks.

Bananas swing from branches high,
Chasing shadows that giggle and lie.
They slip and slide with silly squeals,
Revealing their fruity secret deals.

Fig newtons jump to the funky beat,
While cherries tap dance in bare feet.
The night wears hats of cotton candy,
Where laughter echoes sweet and dandy.

So join the fun, don't be shy,
Each fruit here is a little spry.
The dusk is ripe, the joy is grand,
In this sweet carousel, we'll stand!

Enchanted Citrus Dreams Under Cover of Night

Under a cloak of sparkling sighs,
Citrus critters begin to rise.
Lemon lollipops boast of flair,
Stories spread in the cool night air.

Tangerines waltz with mighty zest,
While limes compete to be the best.
A cloud of giggles floats above,
While tarts prepare for a game of love.

The air is thick with jocular beats,
As oranges dance on tiny feets.
Cupcake towers sway and cheer,
In dreams so sweet, we see them near.

So let the night unfurl its charm,
As fruits come together, free of harm.
In this magical scene, we'll soar,
With sweet delight forevermore!

The Night's Palette of Zestful Hues

A canvas of jolly shades appears,
With paints of laughter, joy, and cheers.
Each slice a verse, each hue a note,
In this zesty boat, we happily float.

Bananas doodle in bright green ink,
While blueberries gust and nod, I think.
Grapefruits giggle with wild delight,
As figs become stars and soar into night.

Lemons draw faces, silly and warm,
Portraying dancing squirrels, a charming swarm.
Pineapples crown themselves with pride,
Amidst colorful fruits them side by side.

So join the fun and lose your frown,
In this fruity fest, we wear our crown.
The night is bright with zestful bliss,
In every splash, a joyful kiss!

Essence of Spicy Citrus Winds

In a grove where oranges dance,
Lemons join the zesty prance,
Limes play tag with tangerines,
Monkey's laughing in between.

Breezy scents of zest and cheer,
Whispers of the fruit appear,
Chasing each with silly glee,
Winding up on top of trees.

Flavors tickle noses well,
Orange peels cast silly spells,
Dressed in fruit like a parade,
Who knew snacks could be this played?

Jokes unfold like peels of zest,
Fruit puns are the very best,
In this orchard, laughter swells,
Where even fruit can crack some shells.

Hidden Garden of Sunburst Secrets

In a garden, sunbeams tease,
Grapefruits giggle in the breeze,
Hidden realms behind a wall,
Where citrus fruits all have a ball.

Lemons in a sneaky plot,
Maybe they can bake a lot?
Orange cakes and limes that sing,
Silly things that fruits can bring.

Sunflowers whisper to the vines,
"Do you think they'll see the signs?"
But fruits just laugh, they're feeling fine,
Joking 'bout their fruity line.

Where tangy jokes weave through the air,
Even bell peppers stop to stare,
In this hidden garden bliss,
Mirthful moments none will miss.

Under the Glow of Tangy Luminescence

Amber lights with citrus flare,
Lemons twirl without a care,
Oranges play their cheeky game,
While pomelos earn their fame.

Glow worms dance in lemon zest,
"Who's the juiciest?" they jest,
Underneath the playful spark,
Fruits shine bright against the dark.

Pineapples pine for limelight's kiss,
Strutting in this fruity bliss,
Tasting laughter, sweet and light,
Chewing on a vine of night.

Witty vibes and jokes abound,
Juggling fruits spin round and round,
Under glow of tangy cheer,
Belly laughs that we hold dear.

Citrus Moonlight and the Spirit's Caress

In moonlit nights, the fruits conspire,
With zest and laughter, they conspire,
A spirit dances with delight,
In joy, they thrive, oh what a sight!

Citrus spirits shake and shake,
Creating laughter, make no mistake,
With winks and giggles, off they soar,
Around the branches, evermore.

Limey sprites with jests galore,
Hiding 'round the old oak door,
They throw a party, loud and bright,
Wishing for a fruity night.

As lemon songs hit every tree,
The world feels light as can be,
With playful spirits' sweet caress,
Fruitful laughter is no less.

Papery Petals and Moonlit Moods

Under glossy leaves, laughter echoes,
Squirrels dance like they're wearing shows.
Crickets sing in silly tunes,
While owls hoot like cartoon loons.

Lemon slices on my nose, oh dear,
Bugs think they're guests, it's very clear.
Moths divebomb in a wobbly flight,
This garden's now a comedy night.

Branching jokes like twisty vines,
Fruit gossip beneath moonshines.
A chicken joins the dance, quite bold,
With polka moves, a sight to behold.

Petals drop as laughter swells,
In moonlit tales, the orchard dwells.
With every giggle, the night grows bright,
A zesty fiesta, a sheer delight.

Tangerine Twilight's Soft Caress

Juicy fruit hangs on laughter's string,
Even frogs around here like to sing.
A tangerine splat on a passing cat,
As squirrels drop nuts like they're in a spat.

Funky fireflies twinkle with cheer,
Tipsy on nectar, they twirl near.
Mice chuckle as they play hide and seek,
In orange-drenched dreams, they sneak a peek.

Grapefruit giggles slip through the leaves,
While bugs wear hats made of soft sheaves.
The breeze whispers jokes from tree to tree,
In this twilight, wild and carefree.

Oh, the moon smiles at their mishaps galore,
As happy fruits roll on the orchard floor.
Each moment a jest, under night's caress,
In this zesty world, nothing's a mess.

Mellow Nights in Orchard Gardens

In orchards where giggles float and sway,
Fruit bats mock with their silly ballet.
Peaches throw shade at passing pears,
While glow-worms dance without any cares.

Cricket comedians host a grand show,
Their punchlines delivered with a bright glow.
A custard apple trips on its own peel,
This night of chuckles is the real deal.

Beneath the leaves, shadows play tag,
Each twirl sending the insects in a brag.
Grapes joke 'bout their juiciness with flair,
Margins of laughter hang thick in the air.

The moon's a noddle, spinning with glee,
Even the lemons join for a big spree.
As soft sighs of fun drift through the space,
Every whimsy finds its rightful place.

The Radiance of the Evening Citrus

Oranges giggle as the sun dips low,
Mandarins gossip, 'Did you see that show?'
A chorus of frogs croak fruity refrains,
While the moon beams down on our zany lanes.

Citrus jokes bob on the warm breeze,
As the hedgehog giggles like it's a tease.
With every squishy fruit on the climb,
The garden's a party, all in good time.

A banana tries a waltz, trips on a root,
Peeling away to start a new shoot.
The raccoons settle with popcorn and smiles,
Sharing tales of their mischievous trials.

Under the glow of this citrusy beam,
The night rolls on, a delightful dream.
With laughter abounding and misfits galore,
Even the stars seem to laugh and explore.

Echoes of Limoncello Dreams

In a garden bright with zest,
Lemons dance, they love to jest.
A squirrel stole a cocktail, you see,
Now he's tipsy, swinging from a tree.

The oranges giggle in the sun,
Poking fun, oh what fun!
A parrot squawks, 'Save me a slice!'
As fruit cocktails chill, oh how nice!

Beneath the stars, the laughter grows,
Citrus jokes are all the pros.
A lime tells a tale of a twisty fate,
While grapefruits snicker, 'You're late, you're late!'

Here comes the chef with a fruity dance,
Banana peels lead a merry prance.
With drinks in hand, we celebrate,
The zesty night that's simply great!

Secrets in the Orchard's Glow

In the orchard, secrets hide,
Lemons winks, and limes are sly.
The oranges share a juicy tale,
While grapefruit trolls will never fail.

A thief in sandals swipes a peach,
As citrus fruits shout, 'Stop! You leech!'
They plot and laugh, and sneak a bite,
While the moon keeps a fruit-saladed sight.

The trees sway gently in the breeze,
As lemon-lovers climb with ease.
Pineapple on the swing, what a sight!
Giggles erupt, oh what pure delight!

Among the branches, jokes abound,
With fruit puns that astound.
Under the glow, all's bright and merry,
With laughter shared, no one is wary!

A Serenade for Golden Orbs

Oh, golden orbs, how you shine so bright,
You roll and tumble, what a silly sight!
With melodies of laughter in the air,
Bananas argue who's the fairest pair.

The tangerines play a musical game,
While limes tell jokes that aren't quite the same.
A pineapple leaps with a twisty twirl,
While lemons watch in a citrus swirl.

In fruit harmony, they do unite,
Strumming guitars in the moon's soft light.
The avocados sing, "Join in our cheer!"
As our friendly orchard party draws near.

With tones of zest and sweet repartee,
These golden orbs bring joy, oh, let it be!
A serenade of flavors, oh what fun,
In this fruity revelry, we all run!

Shadows of the Citrus Grove

In shadows long where citrus play,
Kiting fruits frolic, hip hooray!
A lemon's prank leaves others stunned,
While oranges giggle, pretending to be run.

On the swing, a grapefruit grins,
As laughter erupts, and joy begins.
A lime flips sideways, 'Look! I'm so sly!'
As peels roll laughing, and pineapples fly.

Here in the grove, we share our cheer,
With jokes so zesty, we hold dear.
Each twist and turn brings another laugh,
With every sip of our fruity craft.

So rise and shine, the night is young,
In shadows of laughter, our hearts are strung.
Amongst the tangy joy, we convene,
In the citrus grove, we're all so keen!

The Orange Haze of Midnight

In the garden, fruit does sway,
A rogue squirrel joins the play.
With citrus zest upon his grin,
He's the king where fun begins.

Lemons laugh upon the vine,
While grapefruits sip sweet red wine.
Oranges jive, what a delight!
This crazy dance goes through the night.

Limey tunes fill up the air,
As citrus buddies share a chair.
Citrus dreams just out of reach,
Pop a wedge, now dance and screech!

Underneath the zesty glow,
Those fruits put on a funny show.
With every chuckle, smiles increase,
As we join in their citrus feast!

Citrus-Kissed Memories in the Dark

Fun recollections swirl around,
In the night, laughter's found.
Citrus slices, oh, what joy!
A zany crowd, not just a ploy.

Nostalgia bounces in the breeze,
Lemons rolling, they tease.
Tangerines with perfect aim,
Try to win the fruit toss game!

Jokes are cracked like orange skin,
While funny faces cause a grin.
Sipping juice, our spirits rise,
Underneath the starry skies!

Every shade of citrus cheer,
Dancing with a joyful smear.
Memories wrapped in zany twist,
Who knew fruit could make this list?

Nightfall Over Citrus Fields

As twilight hugs the orchard tight,
Citrus giggles bloom in sight.
Oranges sway with cheeky flair,
"I dare you!" they shout in the air.

A tangerine trip, don't fall down,
The fruit parade goes through the town.
Grapefruits with glasses sing out loud,
"Join our fruity, nutty crowd!"

Beneath the stars, such wild scenes,
Limes in overalls play tambourines.
The moonlight sparkles with delight,
As citrus tops the fun-filled night!

Dancing shadows twist and twirl,
In this crazy, citrus whirl.
With every giggle and late-night zing,
Life feels more like an orange fling!

A Dance of Zesty Shadows

In the moonlight, shadows prance,
Fruity friends join in the dance.
Lemon twirls with dotted flair,
"Watch me, watch me!" fills the air.

Outrageous moves, oh what fun,
Grapefruits bounce, they've just begun.
Kilowatt smiles light the night,
With every spin, they feel so right!

Oranges roll with carefree glee,
Sharing jokes, just let it be.
This funky mix makes spirits soar,
With each zest, we crave for more!

As shadows sway with every beat,
The flavor clash is oh-so-sweet.
Underneath this fruity tune,
We dance away till the break of noon!

Enchanted by Grapefruit Mists

In gardens where the citrus glow,
Grapefruits roll like bowling balls,
Laughter spills, a playful show,
As lemon's zest ignites the halls.

A squirrel dances with delight,
Wearing peels like fanciful hats,
Grapefruit juice in wild flight,
As it slips and slides on mats.

The bees buzz in a buzzing choir,
Sipping nectar like fine wine,
While oranges swing on a high wire,
And laugh at every clumsy line.

With every twist and fruity cheer,
The orchard revels, bright and bold,
In misty air, the fun is clear,
As citrus tales of joy are told.

Twilight Tones of Orchard Bliss

Under the moon, the trees confide,
With oranges all dressed in class,
They giggle softly, side by side,
Creating melodies that surpass.

Lemons play tag with night's soft breeze,
Pretending they're in a grand parade,
While limes roll down with bashful ease,
Laughing at the plans they made.

The grass sprouts jokes in grassy tones,
As every shadow seems to dance,
With grapefruit jokes delivered in groans,
And mournful pears in a funny trance.

In this orchard of fruity glee,
The humor drips like sweetened dew,
With every branch a jubilee,
A silly scene that feels brand new.

A Harvest of Bittersweet Whispers

In twilight's grasp, the fruits convene,
Pears pout as if in secret love,
While grapefruits throw a lively routine,
With wobbly twirls, they leap and shove.

The whispers of lemons, sharp and sly,
Spill tales of sneaky citrus games,
As orange knights on horses high,
Claim glory with their fruity names.

Each apple giggles, pink and round,
As clever puns take flight in style,
While wind chimes hum at the cheerful sound,
Creating a laughter that lasts a while.

Harvest joy and peel the spite,
Sweet sarcasm in nature's jest,
Under stars that twinkle bright,
Sipping juice and feeling blessed.

Saffron Dreams and Citrus Wishes

In saffron shades under the night,
Citrus wishes float like balloons,
With tangerines that shine so bright,
And clementines dancing to tunes.

The grapefruits play hopscotch line,
Laughing at shadows that seem to creep,
While oranges sing in sparkling rhyme,
Spreading smiles a little too deep.

Jokers dressed in vibrant zest,
Spin puns like vines that twist and twirl,
Under the moonlit zestful fest,
Where every fruit's a playful swirl.

As dreams of citrus light the sky,
We dance to the rhythm, free and wide,
With every giggle and silly sigh,
In this orchard, joy's our guide.

Celestial Glow on the Citrus Canopy

Under a sky with a silly grin,
Lemons bouncing in a fruity din.
The stars throw peels with a wink and cheer,
As we dance with laughter, not a single fear.

A grapefruit rolls like a playful cat,
Orange juice rivers in a chatty spat.
We slip on zesty dreams like a slide,
With each wild giggle, we take a ride.

A tangerine tango with a hint of zest,
Citrus critters join, they're the very best.
In this moonlit riot, we can't refrain,
From sharing the spoils of our fruity gain.

So grab a slice and let's take a chance,
In the glow of laughter, we'll prance and dance.
With shining fruit and a comedy show,
We'll toast to the night with a citrus glow.

Chasing Fireflies in the Lemon Grove

Fireflies flicker like lost little stars,
Zipping 'round lemons, they're driving us far.
They giggle and tease, a bright, silly race,
We stumble through trees, both lost in the chase.

Oh how they twinkle, these glowing little gnomes,
Whiskers of laughter in fruity homes.
With tumors of giggles and bellyache glee,
We dance with the night, all wild and free.

Lemonade clouds are pouring from the sky,
As we run after glimmers, forgetting to sigh.
Our feet find the rhythm of a zesty tune,
In the heart of the grove, under laughable moon.

So if you hear chuckles in the citrus-sweet air,
You'll know it's just us—without a care.
Fireflies guide us with their flickering light,
In this grove of lemons, our hearts feel so right.

Starlit Pathways through Fruity Shadows

Down the path where shadows dance,
Fruit flies sing in a lively trance.
A banana slips with a cheeky grin,
As we meander through the fruity din.

Stars above snicker in playful delight,
Peeking through leaves that whisper at night.
With each step we take, our giggles grow loud,
As grapefruit giggles form a fluffy cloud.

Under bright oranges, shadows do sway,
Two lemons conspire to brighten the play.
Oh, what a sight! A starlit parade,
Where laughter and whimsy can never fade.

So wander with me 'neath this fruity scheme,
In shadows of sweetness, we'll live our dream.
With the moon shining down on our zany spree,
Each step is a joke, oh how fun it can be!

Nectar of the Nocturnal Breeze

A breeze whispers secrets of sugar and zest,
Limes chuckle softly, they know they're the best.
The night wears a crown made of citrus delight,
As laughter erupts like a fizzy goodnight.

In a swirl of nectar, we float and we twirl,
Sipping sweet dreams, watch the night unfurl.
Our tongues taste the sparkle of joy in the air,
As giggles pop like bubbles without a care.

The stars join the fun, a cheeky brigade,
In the garden of fruits where mischief is made.
We sip on the breezes, like bubbles of cheer,
As laughter and nectar are all that we hear.

So raise your glass to this playful affair,
To laughter and breezes, we'll dance without care.
With each fruity sip, we spin and we sway,
In the nectar of night, our worries away.

www.ingramcontent.com/pod-product-compliance
Lightning Source LLC
Chambersburg PA
CBHW070314120526
44590CB00017B/2668